MW01286034

Loose Knot

J. Lynden Collingwood

Cover Illustration by:

M. Collingwood

Copyright 2011

ISBN# 978-1-105-83588-9

Maryland, USA

ACKNOWLEDGEMENTS

This has been a journey, but with much joy at the end.

I am forever grateful to Jehovah for making this a reality.

If I was told that 2011 would be a year full of change in my life I may not have believed it.

I would like to thank those who made this possible.

I want to take a moment to thank some key individuals who made this project such a success.

Many thanks to Leon Mensah, who played an important role in

connecting me with two instrumental ladies,

  Who aided my exposure, Stefany Jones and Irene O.

Stefany Jones thanks for allowing my work to be a tool to the hearts of the public.

Thank you for believing in me, my work, and thanks for your patience in guiding me, and creating wings for this project

You are a great mentor.

Thanks to Irene O. for pushing my work out there to the Ghanaian Media and international listeners. Thanks to Sunlight Radio, and Akwaaba Radio for all my interviews and for allowing me the chance to read a poem at Ghana's 54th Independence Day, COGA Party. Wherein, the ambassador of Ghana to the U.S was present. Irene O you are greatly appreciated.

My humble gratitude goes to my sister M. Collingwood who played an important role with the editing and typing of this project, the woman who also put my mind into colors for the cover of the book, and also took my pictures.

Thank you dear, I love you so much.

Also, thanks to Patrice S. Jackson for the help in typing and editing as well.

Thanks to the rest of my family,

My sister Roxanne Collingwood, who has been a great friend to me- thanks for believing in my work.

To my mother, Nmano S. Collingwood my many thanks to you for bringing me this far, without your support I may have not made it.

Thanks to my dad, Jacob M. Collingwood for your love and for being there at times when I was in need.

I am forever grateful to have the experience and privilege of being a father; it has brought me great patience in life, and has given me the respect of God's creation. It has helped mold me into someone different.

When I sometimes feel that things are getting hard in my life that is unbearable, I always remember you boys. I owe it all to you all!

Thank you

Uncle Emmanuel Quaqua; E. A. K. Addy; Loise Bachelerie; Brandon Smith; Maame yaa (Akwaaba radio); Raynada Perry; A. K. Saunders; Yvonne Williams; Rhonda Belt; Sher'ri Williams; Checago Bright-Sawo; Hilary Stryker; Alexis Brown; Amber Williams; Esther Beohourou; Aunty Agnes Thula; Amelia Blackett; Garmai Vazele; Udean Mars; Gormah Kolleh; Reuben Siaka; Maureen Odiatu; Samonee Nimley; Nick Zemura; Nadine Sewell; Mayda Carranza; Miranda Chifamba; Antonio

C.Evangelista; Elodie Bourges; Thera Traore; Claudia Romero; Munah Blackie; Theo Addey; Asha Chaney; Cynthia Jenkins; Ashlee Green (UMUC); Ivan Ikam; Amie Saho; Greta Wilson; Eugenia Paraschis; Prince Nyanti; Toye Cromwell; T. Brown; Cornelia Barnett; Dominique Fontaine; Tenneh Taweh; Sheldon Gills; K. Wall-many thanks. Charles Sumbu; Princess K. Moore; Ria Myles; Erica Ford; Shakia Offutt; Keshaun Winston; Janice Sewell; E.B. Hurley; L.P. Weneah; Debrah Rogers; Fentain Bishop; Idrissa Camara; Their Sow; Olivier Yehou; Canden Webb; David Mzeray; Toyan Williams; Wanga Kamara; Ernestine Clark; Dell Johnny; Jeff Quaye; Jo Morgan; Julian Gbaba-my artists. Thanks to Landry Lignabou-thanks for being there for me at odd times. And thanks to everybody else whom I have encountered along the way- whether it was in the public's eyes or my travels to other countries. To the wonderful people I have met there as well, thank you.

Mr. Kojo Ocran and Mr. Julien Matadi (KP), thanks.

To big brother Lyndon C. Baird, thanks for staying true to me. To my barber Fredie Spry (Next Level), Barber Shop I thank you. To my barber John thanks for being a listening ear. To all my friends who have been true to me along the way- I thank you. To my family and friends in Liberia, to my friends in Ghana and my friends in Ivory Coast and Togo and all over Europe thank you!

To my fans thank you highly for the support. I still have more coming your way.

A note from the author

I have been asked on many occasions, "are you going to first release a book on your life as a child and as an adult now or just poetry first?'' And for quite a while I had no answers because I was clueless……

I began writing at the age of seven and did a play with my sister on my parents' wedding anniversary that year.

My mom said to me that she realized that I had a talent at that age. Not really understanding what it all meant, I reacted as any normal child that age. I said, "oh ok mama" and went on by my business.

I and many others in my country saw a change of life in December 1990 when war broke out and we all were dispersed to other parts of the world. I then saw and experienced things in life that I retained, so then I had even much more love for writing because I was able to express those things on paper. I wanted to get away from all that I had experienced for a while, so I started to look at the brighter side of life. I then decided to write about love. Yes! That love that changes your view of another person. In 2001 I started to write consistently and preserved my work.

Up till now I have written over 5,000 materials on love, war, politics, famine, suffering, homelessness, racism etc…

I found myself writing more poetry on love stories than anything else so I felt that it would be appropriate to release something in the name of love.

My name is J. Lynden Collingwood

I was born and raised partially in Liberia. I am the first born and a brother to two beautiful sisters. I have had the opportunity to live in many other countries and have been able to learn a foreign language and a few dialects during that period. Those experiences and much more have aided me in my work today.

I now live in Montgomery county Maryland- a single man; proud father; a businessman, a prolific writer, poet, (Author) ghost writer, lyricist, Editor, beat composer Music artist management.

I hope you enjoy this book!

My Beautiful Queen

You are the most important part of my life.

You are the greatest, genuine love that has come into my life.

My everyday revolves around you and nothing makes me happier than seeing your pretty smile.

I'm just the humble one and you have taken me for who I am.

I just don't know how to break it down for you, but I cherish you. Even though I may act crazy, but its only love that makes me who I am.

My beautiful queen I have won the noble prize, better yet, a price that is unreachable

Nothing can buy the love that you have for me.

Love Composer

Fruits for desert straight from the harvest land

Beauty placed in your sight.

The light shines from across the room.

Love composer give me keys to compose the love beats that will keep her running back for more.

My body at your bedside ready for dinner taste, evolution of exploring the curves, the figure, the looks, the muscular attraction.

Love composer, the heartbeats introducer, the extension the dimension of how far this love goes, the mental calculator, the thinking mind that stimulates the physical touch to grow butterflies in your stomach.

Love composer, never fall outside of tracks and think that you are in a comfort zone; the least expected, you will be all alone.

So slow down your race and see what's in your face.

Create positive changes, reach states of creating a smooth sailing love composition.

Life Composer

Since then everything has changed, and the skies are so clear, the sun is so bright and my eyes can see the tunnel.

The path is so green and the fruit is so ripe.

The lifetime composer, of true love, that I've been searching for.

Since then and now the smile on my face got me laced up for many more to come.

Your love is certainly one that is worth waiting for.

The joy you bring home is what love is supposed to be

You are a miracle that cannot be explained now or maybe never.

I Thought

I thought I knew love.

I thought love lived close to me.

I thought love and I were so tight.

I thought love and I were bias.

I thought love lived really the love that I lived.

Yes love I'm talking to you.

Why so many changes?

Why whenever I put my hopes up high you let me down?

Why do you keep me so under, facing thunder that hurts so much?

Love, I wanted us to get married but you showed another side of you that caught me off guard.

I thought we could work on things, but you refused to talk... you kept walking, now my life feels so empty. I'm drained out.

Everything seems to be going slow motion.

Love you had it all, but because of your selfishness you wanted things your way.

I thought I knew love.

Breathe In, Breathe Out

Inhale what you can keep; exhale what is so deep.

I inhaled you for many many months, took what I could keep.

I inhaled all the good you gave, and all the bad you did.

I refused and made an excuse just to be with you.

I was sure that our relationship was pure.

I ignored the negativity coming from you and turned that to positivity.

Wherever I went, or whatever I did, I thought about you.

I inhaled every last of you- the body pain, the emotional stress, and the cries.

The lies you told grew old, brought in mill dew and dusted up a few

I choked on but held on when I inhaled so much of you, but when I was ready to exhale I exhaled all of you-the negativity, idiosyncrasies that you delivered to me.

I vomited all, the wasted bad breath that you rubbed off on me.

Please let me be so I can breathe in and out that natural air just to survive another day.

If Tomorrow......

If tomorrow my life changed, and I lost everything that I had, everything that I worked for, would your love be the same?

If tomorrow I was broke

       and could not afford to buy you a bottle of coke

would you consider me to be less of a man?

If tomorrow I could not stand on my feet to feed you because I was paralyzed, would you stay and be by my side, or would you get up and leave?

If tomorrow I got into trouble, would you be able to stick it out for me; or would you say you don't know who I am?

If tomorrow I asked you to get married, would you?

Or would you say no?

Every breath I breathe

Every breath I take is with the help of you.

I breathe love because you motivate me; you are an inspiration to me.

You have inspired me with your life stories... don't worry, as long as I breathe I will make you see love like never before seen.

If our love was not meant to be, where would we be?

I'm satisfied with the breath I breathe because it comes from you.

I'm crazy with this love story; I'm just about over heels with this.

All I want is to please you; I will give you my heart because there is no one else to do this for.

I inhale your love and will continue until you say stop.

All I ask is, let me love you.

Love on Waters

The feeling penetrates my heart and is felt in my toes.

Her voice is the melody that puts me to sleep.

Our connection is of the airwaves.

Her smile is so bright and contagious.

As we speak, we instantly understand and complete each other's sentences.

Her body soft as butter, her smell is of seduction.

Her intelligence is well-designed.

We are in love, yes that love that floats on waters.

Whenever we meet, we greet with butterflies weakening our voices.

Our walks in the park, it's almost like being in a beautiful world.

We greet the birds, meet the squirrels, and say hi to beautiful babies.

Our love on waters gives us the power to make this a smooth sail.

Love on waters, the feeling penetrates my heart and is felt in my toes.

If I say.

If I claimed to love you then my actions should be pure.

I promised to be your strength, your armor, and your protection.

I promised to be your best friend before being your lover.

Somewhere in the midst of all that I forgot all I said to you.

Now the curtains are pulling.

The light is shinning on me as you discover my true colors.

I became a new person right after things got good with us.

I got too comfortable in my space and forgot who I was supposed to stand for.

My deepest apologies to you,

because I ripped your heart away.

If I say I love you, then I should play the cards right.

Icon

Her eyes are a temple of stored graphic memories

Her lips have spoken a thousand languages, expression of her mind

Her brain is a memorized encyclopedia of the past; present meanings that have been locked

Her personality is an expression of a strong woman that never falls short to temptation

She rather will have you thinking a little further than the future

Her legs are kept closed because *precious* is the way she views her body

She is an icon that serves as a concrete to women that are trying to find their path

Hold Me and Love Me

Hold me tight in your arms once again and tell me how deeply you love me.

Whisper in my ears and tell me how this love feels

If love was not sentimental, emotional, and affectionate, where would we be?

This love I share with you cannot be defined in normal terms.

Butterflies....

What a thing that is!

A feeling deep inside that gets you so worked up emotionally when you know and feel that love.

I share every bit of me with you because I know when the morning rises I rise with you

And when the sun shines, I shine with you

And when the stars glow the earth, our relationship glows

When night falls, I fall in love with you again.

Hold me baby. Kiss me baby. Show me that love. Please don't let this be so hard

Open your eyes and see

That you are the only one I breathe

Cherish Her

Love only greets once. . So if you refuse to speak, she politely walks away.

She never pushes you to greet because even though she gets smacked in the face over and over again, she regains strength to move on.

But when you greet her . . . greet her with such respect because this could be the love of your life.

When you find that one that keeps your heart beating faster than the drums, let it be known, it is right to dance to the lovely tune of her heart.

Let her words be a bible to you, a reminder to you as you deal with life on an everyday status.

She deserves everything that is demanded for, because she is here to stay until you turn gray.

If she washes your clothes, cooks dinner, then you have definitely found the winner.

Keep her, because she is truly a keeper!

Now Gone

I sit all by myself, looking back when things were doing so well.

I put my all into it and for a while I was thinking life was good.

There were ups and downs, but I knew we could overcome.

Hurt and pain became our common best friend.

I loved hard but never saw coming what I was blind to.

My emotions were caught up and sometimes reactions were not good.

I seek answers as to why you left with our boys, but only you know.

Now apart for so long, life has been so hard to deal with.

I was hurting, now possibly is, but I can't let that pull me down.

You came back to me wanting this relationship once again.

I almost did not want to give a hearing ear.

I felt that when you came back to me, that you were serious about being back.

If our past is the past, then the present should have been our future.

It did not work out again for us.

I feel this hardness in me, sort of a hit of betrayal

(continued)

But I let my guard down and I got ran over.

     Not mad,

          just don't want to be bothered anymore,

            If it is love she needs,

             then I only hope for her the best.

My love for her,

Man, really just don't know.

It's safe to say that I made such a hard decision that only affected me partially.

This Ring

This ring of 24 karats represents 24 blue seas of beauty

This day is not to be forgotten or mistaken.

This ring symbolizes the full circle of love search that I have finally found.

This ring is my heart to you.

The appreciation of you being there.

Through sunny and rainy days.

You have won my heart over, but look, this is not over.

It has just begun.

I take your hand today, placing a ring on it.

Making you a promise of commitment and trust.

Promising that faithful I will be until the end.

I am marrying you today because it's time to take this relationship to a higher level.

This ring of 24 karats represents the genuine feeling inside of me-making you my wife.

The 24-karats gold represents a full day of traveling across blue seas of beauty

(continued)

Touching down on the mother land where my search of gold
for you,

for a special occasion,

the one standing ovation

giving you that utmost respect.

You are my lady, my queen,

My bride to be.

So let us celebrate and commemorate the appreciation of
your hard work bringing us together

Appreciating one another

Making us a family,

Living for the joy of seeing many other days to flourish.

Your Luv Is My Luv

Your luv is my luv, don't change what we have.

Let luv ride to happiness into the greatness of our lives.

Let laughter always exist even when we grow older.

You know that I luv you until the closure of my eyes,

Nothing stops me from trusting you.

Your beauty cannot be seen in magazines

Your beauty is unique

Pre-t-t-y

Your smile makes me glow.

I will always remember the wonderful and good times we've had.

When you sing to me your voice melts my heart

It puts me in that romance world.

Riches cannot substitute the luv that I have for you.

Riches come and go, but your luv continues to stay

I pray that yesterday and today will be like other days to come.

I cherish you and promise you that I want to live my life with you.

My luv is your luv

and it will continue to be that way.

In My Arms

After the long run baby, I quickly found out that you were not the wrong one.

After the song ends and the instruments lay down to rest,

I will be waiting to receive you with open arms.

So much has happened,

 all I want is you and I putting pieces together making a place of peace.

I sit back and listen to your heart beat so peacefully because we have come to a common ground.

In my arms I hope you will continue to stay; bringing us to harmony.

In my arms will be your comfort for you to run to when you fall weak.

In my arms is where you belong.

Spider Webs

Stuck in the web of confusion,

Need answers, but my questions are numerous.

So where do I dial to get answers?

Life rotating faster than the turns of the globe;

Man, I'm cold... looking for a new view on history.

Relationships, growing into re la-ti-on-spl-it.

No it's not a myth.

Reality keeps shooting bullets at my door.

Sometimes almost refusing to greet her, fearing she may confront me with harder questions.

What could be the worse on sitting on terms that I cannot sign off on?

Speaking of truth, looking for that girl named Ruth,

Maybe she is just my truth.

I bargain with consequences after it's all done and I find myself against the wall looking so stupid.

You take chances; you lose your identity of self-consciousness.

Life is a ride, so when born; you're married to her or him; however you view your sexuality.

(continued)

But life never changes preference in whom she dates and who gets it the most.

Man, you have to cope,

It's not just dope that makes you high.

It's your mistakes that give you inspiration to life.

You have to have met her; she is your life-long-time partner.

Don't run a marathon to see or feel life,

Step out the door and she will drop you to the floor.

Yes, cold she can be.

Speak of facts because I owe you nothing.

Speak up through your speakers and I will speak about her.

Each Day

She is sweeter than roses on an evening of romance.

Beauty lies in her hands.

There is not a day I don't thank her for being there for me.

Through the ups and downs; the falls, the growing up, she has stuck by my side.

The time is right, so it's only fair that she gets what she always expected.

Each day your love grows twice bigger than the day before.

Each day the sweet bloom blooms in her bedroom.

Sunrise watching her belly grows to a perfect round moon.

This is history in the making. . Each day her love deepens for me

Each day is greater perfection.

Nothing but Smiles

I now realize the meaning of having you.

Every touch is an object that keeps a feeling that penetrates deep inside

This life is so pure.

Your reach has touched me so much, and I take the best out of it

Leave now or stay, I prefer to keep this love thing going.

Your love comes naturally, magical; your actions speak greatly than words

So my emotions have come to a full extension

So I now know that nothing separates us.

Today or tomorrow, through any sorrow, the Creator has put us together

So like birds, we use our feathers to fly into a universe of no course

I Can Do It Again

If you give me the chance I promise I can do it again,

    If so, even better

Yes I told you things would change, and time is the only wait that keeps us waiting

I am doing this all over again just to regain the trust that stepped out our doors.

I'm not afraid to admit that my actions are part of the reason why this is at a standstill

Try and put your heart into it again, and believe me there will be changes

Sorry can't break the silence, but promises will be fulfilled

I can do it again.

Where there is Love

Love runs like water

      Grabbing it feels like smooth leather

If love runs pure, you will know.

      When you stick around, you will get that stable ground of stability.

Attraction is fatal, but love is vital.

      You see her and you feel your heart belongs to her.

You treat her as a queen; bring her a new love scene.

      Your kisses, hugs, and smiles make a difference.

Your ears are a special tool-you learn to listen and appreciate her soft voice

      Even when it seems like she is not making sense

You just give her that pleasure to make her presence felt

      Love is like honey. When you pour, it spreads all over and covers every spot

Love is alike. You spread your love and make it go all the way around

      Where there is love, there is trust, devotion, new creation, faithfulness, joy, and hope

Where there is love,

      There is love.

Romance. . . Road Ends

She says *romance*,

I say back to her: The romance ends right at the exit sign.

Tired of romance, tired of putting so much time into something that has no meaning

She says *romance*,

And I say don't expect me to do what you want.

This is my time, my rhymes.

If we dance to it, then we will romance to it.

My romance, road ends; take those ends; make a cent out of a penny.

Location of love, there is no rotation.

Love ends; love has been spent; love cannot be turned around.

Love becomes evil.

It's an emergency and I have to get back on the road.

A new road that will start a new life.

Romance me,

Romance see

Just for the last time, there is no forgiveness.

Forget the rest

But life goes on.

Shredded Heart

All in it! All about it!

Sacrifice, yes, to the endless stop!

Tears of fear, mixed in with joy

Tears of having the completion of you by my side

But knowing the smiles you smile are never the greatest

You put yourself in a position to compliment the relationship

But sometimes you ask if the tries, the fights, the cries, the extra mile that was given was worth the try

I'm broken into pieces that cannot be put together

My hope quickly fading away

The trust of being sure it's working out has been out the door long ago.

My heart is displaced not because I want it to, but because it's so much to hold back just to keep track

Love compliments the weather

Yes, nothing too sweet

Yes I've met the sour, sweet side and its nothing too pretty

Shredded heart. . . Stop doing this to me.

Your World

Baby, this world is yours, and anything you ask for will be given
Your world is the definition of happiness
Your world is a place of peace of mind
Your world is a world without the worries
A place, a setting of relaxation
Your world is a day without cries
But rather a 24-hour zone of laughter
Your world is full of beauty, kindness, and joy
Your world is full of fulfillment and accomplishments
Your world is a world that many dream of but cannot see
Your world is our world and you are the reason my world is content

Losing You. . . to the World

When you looked at me and said: baby I'm out the door;

I thought it was just like all the other times.

Multiple times you went out the door but always returned.

Your attitude reached up an altitude.

But I memorized exactly the time you would walk back through the door.

Now, you're gone. There is no one to keep me company, fuss, and fight with.

I realized you were gone when I had not seen you after a day or two.

I kept my emotions that I had far within

Never told you how much I loved you

Never kissed

But was always ready to diss

I miss you even though you're long gone to another world of another man loving and caring for you.

Baby I'm a changed man now; I don't know how to explain this to you...

Baby. Baby? *Please* hear me out.

Don't tear me out

Because I know I was wrong

But I still need you

I want to restart from the top and end at the bottom.

Baby! I love you! I want to kiss you, never dissing you!

But I know my words have no meanings to you anymore. . .

Hoping for a Closure

Complete closure possibilities seem very slim.

A mind set free, hoping to let go of hurt.

Closure to questions, from me that have not been answered.

I feel stacked in a suitcase always on the run, refusing to sit and discuss face to face our differences in our lives.

I've tried to put an end to confusions, blames, aims of hurt.

Sometimes I feel very close to discussing, but then I'm pushed away as if I became your worst enemy.

We look the same, breathe the same, but don't think or see things the same.

I'm a spitting image of you. When I see you my mind run back to the images, yes, the dark images that others don't know about, who are you; who caused you to become someone different today?

Why do you keep a distance? What are your deep dark dirty secrets?

The stage is there; lights on. Speak up and don't be afraid to tell the truth.

Your Equivalence

There is no where in this world I could go and find a currency as high as yours, even money exchangers ask me why waste their time coming to them teasing them with this high equivalence.

There is no comparison indeed as to your rich qualities that you possess.

I've been around the world looking for true equivalence; an equivalence that no human could exchange for something else; an equivalence that no one could touch or feel or move. It's been years to come, not really getting what I wanted. Today I can say I hold on to an equivalence that is even better than what I had, there's no comparison to you and others because yours is very different, very pure and very adequate.

Your equivalence is one to hold on to and not foolishly let go, letting someone else receive what I can keep.

I cherish you everyday and it is something I can never forget; it remains here and forever.

When love strikes

I had it all and some more but I guess I took things for granted.

I am now considered your number one worst enemy, but reality my heart is given.

When loves bites, it sucks away all hopes.

So here I am trying to cope, that makes my life so complicated.

My mind is frozen my heart hotter then an oven.

It was once a family but now things have changed, so here still living with her but viewed as nothing.

I've become the stranger in her home so the doors are awaiting my exit.

We have a child together that's on the way but our child will live in a broken home.

This hurts me so much- all I really wanted was for us to be together.

Not Long Before

Before we act stupid let's sit and discuss our problems. Break it down for me and speak your mind, and let me sincerely know how hard it is for you.

Let's not act stupid and decide to let it go. Before we break down and lose hope, hopefully we can work on things to improve the love that is still intense. Let's not make the little things disturb the structure of love that has been built.

Not too long after did we realize was that what was here, was meant to be. But what's out that door is just a second too late to regret. This love is quickly slipping away from us.

Let's develop on our love and make it stronger

NOT SO OFTEN

Not so often does your love come around.

Speakers' sounds, deeper on my drums, reminding me of this life

Not so often do you find stability at an early age.

Wisdom carries your weight a long way

Sometimes carried away with your love

Caught up with you, not so often a smile so bright presents itself

My love, you never cease to amaze me, your love comes so colorful.

You softly soak me in.

Not so often does it happen this way.

So I can only accept you for what you really are

Our love does rhyme, giving in to time, as we see the positive changes

that suitably fits us perfectly.

Not so often does your love come around

ONLY YOU

Only your love makes me so content
Many men may try to be me
But your love continues to make me glow
So when they see me they're enraged
Only your love makes me so content
Ever since I met you my queen
I could feel the love wind
Nobody has made me feel so weak.
 So I do all in my strength to show you, the love within.
Baby you are part of my sweet history
You look so great and there is nothing greater
than you being my mate.
 Only your love makes me so content
Many men may try to be me
But you have made me a part of your team
Only you, only you, yes only you

MISS LADY

You are looking so fly
Can I take a walk with you?
Whisper in your ears few seductive things
Expressions on how I feel about you.
Can I hold your hands, and look into your eyes
And watch your smile?
Can I give you a kiss, on your lips?
As I taste your sweetness
Can we fall in love at first sight, avoid the fights
And just get into each other's sight.
Can I make you my lady, can I be your save haven
Can I protect you at all times?
May I cherish the grounds you walk on?
Can we talk more often than just this hour?
You are looking so fly, baby
Can I fly with you?

DEEP DOWN MY SOUL

Deep down in my soul is this love I feel for you

Your presence has me in a daze

Deep down in my soul

You make me feel so brand new

Love has never felt so strong

And I know it's not wrong

to feel so deep about you

Ooh I feel this deep down in my toes,

The sensation so out of control

Baby you have my heart melting

By the way you speak to me, your voice so soft,

Almost feeling like cotton candy

This love ooh this love is felt so deep down in my soul

Your gracious purity, has me deep in love with you

Deep down in my soul is this love I feel for you

Your presence has me in a daze

Deep down in my soul

CAN'T GET ENOUGH

Honey drops into my mind set

Sweetened to your taste

Voices soothing to my heart

Addicted to your love, sometimes really sinning,

 going overboard in wanting more,more of your kindness,

 the picture you have shown me, the path of where you walk.

They may talk about us, but nothing they say carries any kind of weight.

Temptations may visit our hearts but only if wanted, then allowed.

I'm into and all over you, your love has a ringtone that I cannot erase

Really wanting this to be more than just today,

But a promising future.

Your love has melted a hard side of me.

Honey drops into my mind set

Sweetened to your taste

Voices soothing to my heart

LOVE ON WINGS

Baby… baby your love is smoother than any path.

You have made me see your love from another angle,

An eye is open so outspoken

You break things down to me step by step

Love on wings and you have me flying higher than average

My heart is wrapped around you and nothing really matters

Hooked on your personality, something so refreshing

Love on wings, love on a higher level.

Thanks to God for bringing me something so brand new

So my clothes have no value, because I keep wearing your love every day.

I'm deep in love with you and this is no metaphor, but true love that has reached my heart.

Baby baby your love is smoother than any paved path

Even when I'm in the wrong, you never come of disrespectful to me

You keep this love coming

So I can't stop talking about you

You are so sweet; let me drink the reality of your love

IN HER WORDS

Words through speakers, grasped my attention, a tone so unfamiliar

But sweeter than ice cream comb,

 Dripping,

 With metaphors.

A new birth of sounds that no music composer has ever mastered

Yesterday a new life out of earth's creation

Her whispers flow purely as a water fountain located in a quiet place in the park

She softly speaks, no forceful effort, she breaks barriers in me,

Melting me down to sugar.

She is sweet and eatable her personality strikes me with a sudden silence,

that freezes me in a puzzle, trying to figure out how all the pieces fit in perfectly.

She came unexpectedly, yes my dream in a manner so on time

Words through speakers,

 her action selfishly lethal,

 but more entertaining than any classics.

And now she got me changing lanes, speed so unstoppable

Crazy insane, insane crazy, love is within

So no control on my deep feelings, now weakened, but strengthened by her words.

Something so unfamiliar is what's knocking at my door